Nautical Terms

A Dictionary

David Tuffley

To my beloved Nation of Four
Concordia Domi – Foris Pax

i

Published 2013 by Altiora Publications

ISBN-13: 978-1495267819

The author gratefully acknowledges the source of this glossary that explicitly allows
its use here under the terms of *Creative Commons Attribution-ShareAlike 3.0
Unported License.* http://creativecommons.org/licenses/by-sa/3.0/

About the Author
David Tuffley PhD is an academic at Griffith University in Australia. When he is
not working, he likes nothing better than getting out on the water. The East
Coast of Australia where David lives has some of the finest freshwater, inshore
and offshore boating opportunities in the world.

Acknowledgements

I acknowledge my family upbringing that taught the joy of messing about in boats.
My father and older brothers all have salt water in their veins, and so do I.

A

Aback: A sail that has the wind pressing on its forward surface, pushing the vessel backward. Also describes the dangerous situation of a square-rigged vessel accidentally sailing with the wind on the wrong side of its sails.

Abaft: Toward the stern, relative to some object ('abaft the fore hatch').

Abeam: On the beam, a relative bearing at right angles to the centreline of the ship's keel.

Aboard: On or in a vessel (see also 'close aboard').

Above board: On or above the deck, in plain view, not hiding anything.

Above-water hull: The hull section of a vessel above the waterline, the visible part of a ship. Also, topsides.

Accommodation ladder: A portable flight of steps down a ship's side.

Admiralty: A government department administering naval affairs; also refers to the court having jurisdiction over maritime law and disputes.

Adrift: Afloat and unattached in any way to the shore or seabed, but not under way. It implies that a vessel is not under control and therefore goes where the wind and current take her (loose from moorings, or out of place). Also refers to any gear not fastened down or put away properly. It can also be used to mean 'absent without leave'.

Afloat: Of a vessel which is floating freely (not aground or sunk). More generally of vessels in service ('the company has 10 ships afloat').

Afore: 1. In, on, or toward the front of a vessel. 2. In front of a vessel.

Aft: 1. The portion of the vessel behind the middle area of the vessel. 2. Towards the stern (of the vessel).

Afternoon watch: The 1200–1600 watch.

Aground: Resting on or touching the ground or bottom (usually involuntarily).

Ahead: Forward of the bow.

Ahoy: A cry to draw attention. Term used to hail a boat or a ship, as 'Boat ahoy!'

Alee: 1. On the lee side of a ship. 2. To leeward.

All hands: Entire ship's company, both officers and enlisted personnel.

Aloft: In the rigging of a sailing ship. Above the ship's uppermost solid structure; overhead or high above.

Alongside: By the side of a ship or pier.

Amidships (or midships): In the middle portion of ship, along the line of the keel.

Anchor: 1. an object designed to prevent or slow the drift of a ship, attached to the ship by a line or chain; typically a metal, hook-like or plough-like object designed to grip the bottom under the body of water (but also see sea anchor). 2. to deploy an anchor ('She anchored offshore.')

Anchorage: A suitable place for a ship to anchor. Area of a port or harbor.

Anchor's aweigh: Said of an anchor when just clear of the bottom.

Apparent wind: The wind experienced by a moving vessel, being the combination of the true wind and the headwind created by the vessel's own forward movement through the air.

As the crow flies: A direct line between two points (which might cross land) which is the way crows travel rather than ships which must go around land.

Avast: Stop, cease or desist from whatever is being done. From the Dutch hou' vast ('hold fast'), from houd ('hold') + vast ('fast').

Awash: So low in the water that the water is constantly washing across the surface.

Aweigh: Position of an anchor just clear of the bottom.

B

Backstays: Long lines or cables, reaching from the stern of the vessel to the mast heads, used to support the mast.

Baggywrinkle: A soft covering woven from old rope yarns and wrapped around standing rigging to prevent sails from chafing against the wire or rope.

Bailer: A device for removing water that has entered the boat.

Ballast: Heavy material — stone, iron, lead, sand, or water — placed low in a vessel's hull to lower the centre of gravity and improve stability.

Ballast tank: A device used on ships and submarines and other submersibles to control buoyancy and stability

Bank: A large area of elevated sea floor.

Bar: Large mass of sand or earth, formed by the surge of the sea. They are mostly found at the entrances of great rivers or havens, and often render navigation extremely dangerous, but confer tranquillity once inside. See also: Touch and go, grounding. Alfred Lord Tennyson's poem 'Crossing the bar' is an allegory for death.

Bareboat charter: An arrangement for the chartering or hiring of a vessel, whereby the vessel's owner provides no crew or provisions as part of the agreement; instead, the people who rent the vessel are responsible for crewing and provisioning her.

Barge: 1. A towed or self-propelled flat-bottomed boat, built mainly for river, canal, and coastal transport of heavy goods. 2. Admiral's barge: A boat at the disposal of an admiral for his or her use as transportation between a larger vessel and the shore or within a harbour.

Batten: A thin, flexible strip of wood or fibreglass inserted into a pocket sewn into the leech of a sail to help it hold its designed shape and prevent flutter.

Beaching: Deliberately running a vessel aground to load and unload (as with landing craft), or sometimes to prevent a damaged vessel sinking.

Beacon: A lighted or unlighted fixed aid to navigation attached directly to the earth's surface. (Lights and day beacons both constitute beacons.)

Beam: The width of a vessel at the widest point, or a point alongside the ship at the midpoint of its length.

Beam ends: The sides of a ship. 'On her beam ends' may mean the vessel is literally on her side and possibly about to capsize; more often, the phrase means the vessel is listing 45 degrees or more.

Bear down or bear away: Turn away from the wind, often with reference to a transit.

Bearing: The horizontal direction of a line of sight between two objects on the surface of the earth. See also 'absolute bearing' and 'relative bearing'.

Beating or Beat to: Sailing as close as possible towards the wind (perhaps only about 60°) in a zig-zag course to attain an upwind direction to which it is impossible to sail directly.(also tacking)

Beaufort scale: The scale describing wind force devised by Admiral Sir Francis Beaufort in 1808, in which winds are graded by the effect of their force (originally, the amount of sail that a fully rigged frigate could carry). Scale now reads up to Force 17.

Becalm: To cut off the wind from a sailing vessel, either by the proximity of land or by another vessel.

Becalmed: Unable to move due to lack of wind; said of a sailing vessel.

Belay: 1. To make fast a line around a fitting, usually a cleat or belaying pin. 2. To secure a climbing person in a similar manner. 3. An order to halt a current activity or countermand an order prior to execution.

Bend: A knot used to join two ropes together or to secure a rope to a fixed object such as a spar or ring. Common bends include the sheet bend and the carrick bend.

Berth (moorings): A location in a port or harbour used specifically for mooring vessels while not at sea.

Berth (navigation): Safety margin of distance to be kept by a vessel from another vessel or from an obstruction, hence the phrase, 'to give a wide berth.'scribd

Berth (sleeping): A bed or sleeping accommodation on a boat or ship.

Bilge: The compartment at the bottom of the hull of a ship or boat where water collects and must be pumped out of the vessel.

Bilge keels: A pair of keels on either side of the hull, usually slanted outwards. In yachts, they allow the use of a drying mooring, the boat standing upright on the keels (and often a skeg) when the tide is out.

Bimini top: Open-front canvas top for the cockpit of a boat, usually supported by a metal frame.

Binnacle: The stand on which the ship's compass is mounted.

Bitter end: The last part or loose end of a rope or cable. The anchor cable is tied to the bitts; when the cable is fully paid out, the bitter end has been reached.

Block: A pulley or set of pulleys.

Blue Peter: A blue and white flag (the flag for the letter 'P') hoisted at the foretrucks of ships about to sail. Formerly a white ship on a blue ground, but later a white square on a blue ground.

Boatswain: A non-commissioned officer responsible for the sails, ropes, rigging and boats on a ship who issues 'piped' commands to seamen.

Bobstay: A heavy stay running from the end of the bowsprit down to the waterline at the stem, counteracting the upward pull of the forestay on the bowsprit end.

Bollard: From 'bol' or 'bole', the round trunk of a tree. A substantial vertical pillar to which lines may be made fast.

Booby: A type of bird that has little fear and therefore is particularly easy to catch.

Boom: A spar attached to the foot of a fore-and-aft sail.

Bosun's chair: A seat or harness used to hoist a crew member aloft up the mast for inspection or repair work.

Bow: The forward-most part of a vessel's hull, designed to cut through the water.

Bow thruster: A small propeller or water-jet at the bow, used for manoeuvring larger vessels at slow speed. May be mounted externally, or in a tunnel running through the bow from side to side.

Bowline: 1. One of the most useful knots in seamanship, forming a fixed, non-slipping loop at the end of a rope. 2. (Historical) A line used to hold the weather leech of a square sail forward and prevent it from being blown back.

Bowsprit: A spar projecting forward from the bow of a vessel, to which the forestays are attached, allowing headsails to be set further forward.

Boxing the compass: To state all 32 points of the compass, starting at north, proceeding clockwise. Sometimes applied to a wind that is constantly shifting.

Breakwater: 1. A structure constructed on a coast as part of a coastal defense system or to protect an anchorage from the effects of weather and longshore drift. 2. A structure built on the forecastle of a ship intended to divert water away from the forward superstructure or gun mounts.

Bridge: A structure above the weather deck, extending the full width of the vessel, which houses a command centre, itself called by association, the bridge.

Broach: When a sailing vessel loses control of its motion and is forced into a sudden sharp turn, often heeling heavily and in smaller vessels sometimes leading to a capsize. The change in direction is called broaching-to. Occurs when too much sail is set for a strong gust of wind, or in circumstances where the sails are unstable.

Bulwark (or Bulward): The extension of the ship's side above the level of the weather deck.

Bunk: A fixed sleeping berth built into the hull structure of a vessel.

Buoy: A floating object of defined shape and colour, which is anchored at a given position and serves as an aid to navigation.

By the lee: A point of sailing on which the wind comes from the same side as the boom; a dangerous situation as it can cause an accidental and violent gybe.

C

Cabin: an enclosed room on a deck or flat.

Cable length: A measure of length or distance. Equivalent to (UK) 1/10 nautical mile, approx. 600 feet; (USA) 120 fathoms, 720 feet (219 m); other countries use different values.

Canal boat: A specialized watercraft designed for operation on a canal.

Canoe stern: A design for the stern of a yacht which is pointed, like a bow, rather than squared off as a transom.

Cape Horn fever: The name of the fake illness a malingerer is pretending to suffer from.

Capsize: When a ship or boat lists too far and rolls over, exposing the keel. On large vessels, this often results in the sinking of the ship.

Capstan: A large winch with a vertical axis. A full-sized human-powered capstan is a waist-high cylindrical machine, operated by a number of hands who each insert a horizontal capstan bar in holes in the capstan and walk in a circle. Used to wind in anchors or other heavy objects; and sometimes to administer flogging over.

Careening: Tilting a ship on its side, usually when beached, to clean or repair the hull below the water line. Also known as to 'heave down'.

Cat o' nine tails: A short nine-tailed whip kept by the bosun's mate to flog sailors (and soldiers in the Army). When not in use, the cat was kept in a baize bag, hence the term 'cat out of the bag'. 'Not enough room to swing a cat' also derives from this.

Caulk: To seal the seams between the planks of a wooden hull with oakum and tar (or modern compounds) to prevent water ingress and keep the vessel watertight.

Centreboard: A board or plate lowered through the hull of a dinghy on the centreline to resist leeway.

Chafing: Wear on line or sail caused by constant rubbing against another surface.

Chafing gear: Material applied to a line or spar to prevent or reduce chafing.

Chart: A nautical map used for navigation at sea, showing coastlines, water depths, hazards, tidal information, and the positions of navigational aids.

Chart table: The designated workspace aboard a vessel where the navigator lays out, studies, and stores charts and other navigational publications.

Chine: The line or edge where the bottom of the hull meets the topsides (the side of the hull). A 'hard chine' is an abrupt angle; a 'soft chine' is a rounded transition.

Chock-a-block: Rigging blocks that are so tight against one another that they cannot be further tightened.

Chronometer: A timekeeper accurate enough to be used to determine longitude by means of celestial navigation.

Clean bill of health: A certificate issued by a port indicating that the ship carries no infectious diseases. Also called a pratique.

Clean slate: At the helm, the watch keeper would record details of speed, distances, headings, etc. on a slate. At the beginning of a new watch the slate would be wiped clean.

Cleat: A stationary device used to secure a rope aboard a vessel.

Clew: The lower aft corner of a fore-and-aft sail, to which the sheet is attached. On a square sail, the two lower corners are both called clews.

Close-hauled: The point of sailing in which a vessel is steered as close to the direction of the wind as it can effectively sail, with sails trimmed in tight.

Coaming: The raised edge of a hatch, cockpit or skylight to help keep out water.

Coaster (or coastal trading vessel): A shallow-hulled ship used for trade between locations on the same island or continent.

Cockpit: The seating area (not to be confused with Deck). The area towards the stern of a small decked vessel that houses the rudder controls.

Companionway: A raised and windowed hatchway in the ship's deck, with a ladder leading below and the hooded entrance-hatch to the main cabins.

Complement: The number of persons in a ship's crew, including officers.

Counter: The overhanging section of the stern projecting aft and above the waterline.

Crosstrees: two horizontal struts at the upper ends of the topmasts of sailboats, used to anchor the shrouds from the topgallant mast.

Crow's nest: Specifically a masthead constructed with sides and sometimes a roof to shelter the lookouts from the weather, generally by whaling vessels, this has become a generic term for what is properly called masthead. See masthead.

Cut and run: When wanting to make a quick escape, a ship might cut lashings to sails or cables for anchors, causing damage to the rigging, or losing an anchor, but shortening the time needed to make ready by bypassing the proper procedures.

Cut of his jib: The 'cut' of a sail refers to its shape. Since this would vary between ships, it could be used both to identify a familiar vessel at a distance, and to judge the possible sailing qualities of an unknown one. Also used figuratively of people.

D

Daggerboard: A type of light centreboard that is lifted vertically; often in pairs, with the leeward one lowered when beating.

Davit: 1. A spar formerly used on board ships as a crane to hoist the flukes of the anchor to the top of the bow, without injuring the sides of the ship. 2. A crane, often working in pairs and usually made of steel, used to lower things over the side of a ship, including launching a lifeboat over the side of a ship.

Davy Jones' Locker: An idiom for the bottom of the sea.

Day-blink: Moment at dawn where, from some point on the mast, a lookout can see above low lying mist which envelops the ship.

Dead in the water: Not moving (used only when a vessel is afloat and neither tied up nor anchored).

Dead reckoning: The process of calculating a vessel's current position based on a previously known position, then advancing that position using estimated speed, heading, and time elapsed, without external navigational fixes.

Deck hand or decky: A person whose job involves aiding the deck supervisor in (un)mooring, anchoring, maintenance, and general evolutions on deck.

Deck supervisor: The person in charge of all evolutions and maintenance on deck; sometimes split into two groups: forward deck supervisor, aft deck supervisor.

Decks: The top of the boat; the surface is removed to accommodate the seating area. The structures forming the approximately horizontal surfaces in the ship's general structure. Unlike flats, they are a structural part of the ship.

Decks awash: A situation in which the deck of the vessel is partially or wholly submerged, possibly as a result of excessive listing or a loss of buoyancy.

Depth sounder: An electronic instrument that measures the depth of water beneath a vessel by timing the return of a sound pulse from the seabed; also called an echo sounder.

Devil to pay (or Devil to pay, and no pitch hot): 'Paying' the devil is sealing the devil seam. It is a difficult and unpleasant job (with no resources) because of the shape of the seam (up against the stanchions) or if the devil refers to the garboard seam, it must be done with the ship slipped or careened.

Dinghy: 1. A type of small boat, often carried or towed as a ship's boat by a larger vessel. 2. Also a small racing yacht or recreational open sailing boat, often used for beginner training rather than sailing full-sized yachts. 3. Utility dinghies are usually rowboats or have an outboard motor, but some are rigged for sailing.

Displacement: The weight of water displaced by the immersed volume of a ship's hull, exactly equivalent to the weight of the whole ship.

Displacement hull: A hull designed to travel through the water, rather than planing over it.

Distinguishing mark: A flag flown to distinguish ships of one seagoing service of a given country from ships of the country's other seagoing service(s) when ships of more than one of the country's seagoing services fly the same ensign.

Dock: 1. In American usage, a fixed structure attached to shore to which a vessel is secured when in port, generally synonymous with pier and wharf, except that pier tends to refer to structures used for tying up commercial ships and to structures extending from shore for use in fishing, while dock refers more generally to facilities used for tying up ships or boats, including recreational craft. 2. In British usage, the body of water between two piers or wharves which accommodates vessels tied up at the piers or wharves. 3. To tie up along a pier or wharf.

Dodger: A canvas or clear vinyl spray shield fitted at the forward end of the cockpit to protect the crew from spray, wind, and rain.

Dog watch: A short watch period, generally half the usual time (e.g. a two-hour watch rather than a four-hour one). Such watches might be included in order to rotate the system over different days for fairness, or to allow both watches to eat their meals at approximately normal times.

Doldrums or equatorial calms: The equatorial trough, with special reference to the light and variable nature of the winds.youtube

Downhaul: A line used to control either a mobile spar, or the shape of a sail. A downhaul can also be used to retrieve a sail back on deck.

Draft: The vertical distance between the waterline and the lowest point of the keel; the minimum water depth required for a vessel to float. Also spelled 'draught'.

Drogue: A device to slow a boat down in a storm so that it does not speed excessively down the slope of a wave and crash into the next one. It is generally constructed of heavy flexible material in the shape of a cone. Also see sea anchor.

Dunnage: 1. Loose packing material used to protect a ship's cargo from damage during transport. (Also see #Fardage) 2. Personal baggage.

E

Earings: Small lines, by which the uppermost corners of the largest sails are secured to the yardarms.

East Indiaman: Any ship operating under charter or license to any of the East India Companies of Denmark, England, France, the Netherlands, Portugal, Sweden, or the United Kingdom from the 17th to the 19th century.

Ebb tide: The period of the tidal cycle during which the tide is receding and sea levels are falling.

Echo sounding: Measuring the depth of the water using a sonar device.

Embayed: The condition where a sailing vessel (especially one which sails poorly to windward) is confined between two capes or headlands by a wind blowing directly onshore.

Eye splice: A closed loop or eye at the end a line, rope, cable etc. It is made by unravelling its end and joining it to itself by intertwining it into the lay of the line. Eye splices are very strong and compact and are employed in moorings and docking lines among other uses.

F

Fairlead: A fitting — ring, block, or cleat — used to guide a line in a specific direction, keeping it clear of obstructions and preventing chafe.

Fairwater: A structure that improves the streamlining of a vessel.

Fantail: Aft end of the ship, also known as the Poop deck.

Fathom: A unit of length equal to 6 feet (1.8 m), roughly measured as the distance between a man's outstretched hands. Particularly used to measure depth.

Fender: A protective bumper, usually made of rubber, foam, or vinyl, hung over the side of a vessel to absorb impact and prevent damage when lying alongside a dock or another vessel.

Figurehead: A symbolic image at the head of a traditional sailing ship or early steamer.

First mate: The second-in-command of a commercial ship.

Fitting-out: The period after a ship is launched during which all the remaining construction of the ship is completed and she is readied for sea trials and delivery to her owners.

Fixed propeller: A propeller mounted on a rigid shaft protruding from the hull of a vessel, usually driven by an inboard motor; steering must be done using a rudder. See also outboard motor and stern drive.

Flagship: 1. A vessel used by the commanding officer of a group of naval ships (reflecting the custom of its commander, characteristically a flag officer, flying a distinguishing flag aboard the ship on which he or she is embarked. 2. Used more loosely, the lead ship in a fleet of naval or commercial vessels, typically the first, largest, fastest, most heavily armed, or, in terms of media coverage, best-known.

Flood tide: The period of the tidal cycle during which the tide is rising and sea levels are increasing.

Flotsam: Debris or cargo that remains afloat after a shipwreck. See also jetsam.

Fly by night: A large sail used only for sailing downwind, requiring little attention.

Following sea: Wave or tidal movement going in the same direction as a ship

Foot: The bottom edge of a sail, running between the tack and the clew.

Fore: Toward, at, or near the bow of a vessel.

Fore-and-aft: Running along the length of the vessel, parallel to the keel; used to describe the alignment of sails, rigging, or fittings.

Forecastle: A partial deck, above the upper deck and at the head of the vessel; traditionally the sailors' living quarters. Pronounced /ˈfoʊksəl/. The name is derived from the castle fitted to bear archers in time of war.

Forestays: Long lines or cables, reaching from the bow of the vessel to the mast heads, used to support the mast.

Freeboard: The distance measured from the waterline to the top of the deck at its lowest point; the portion of the hull that is above the water.

Furl: To roll or gather a sail against its mast or spar.

G

Gaff rigged: A boat rigged with a four-sided fore-and-aft sail with its upper edge supported by a spar or gaff which extends aft from the mast.

Galley: The kitchen or cooking area of a vessel.

Gangplank: A movable bridge used in boarding or leaving a ship at a pier; also known as a 'brow'.

Gangway: An opening in the bulwark of the ship to allow passengers to board or leave the ship.

Gennaker: A large, lightweight sail used for sailing a fore-and-aft rig down or across the wind, intermediate between a genoa and a spinnaker.

Genoa or genny: A large jib, strongly overlapping the mainmast.

Ghost: To sail slowly when there is apparently no wind.

Gig (Captain's gig): A boat on naval ships at the disposal of the ship's captain for his or her use in transportation to other ships or to the shore.

Gin-pole: A pole that is attached perpendicular to the mast, to be used as a lever for raising the mast. Also jin-pole.

Give-way (vessel): Where two vessels are approaching one another so as to involve a risk of collision, this is the vessel which is directed to keep out of the way of the other.

Glass: A marine barometer. (Older barometers used mercury-filled glass tubes to measure and indicate barometric pressure.)

Global Positioning System: (GPS) A satellite based radio navigation system providing continuous worldwide coverage. It provides navigation, position, and timing information to air, marine, and land users.

Going about or tacking: Changing from one tack to another by going through the wind (see also gybe).

Gooseneck: Fitting that attaches the boom to the mast, allowing it to move freely.

Grave: To clean a ship's bottom.

Graving dock: A narrow basin, usually made of earthen berms and concrete, closed by gates or by a caisson, into which a vessel may be floated and the water pumped out, leaving the vessel supported on blocks; the classic form of dry-dock.

Grog: Watered-down purser's rum consisting of half a gill with equal part of water, issued to all seamen over twenty. (CPOs and POs were issued with neat rum) From the British Admiral Vernon who, in 1740, ordered the men's ration of rum to be watered down. He was called 'Old Grogram' because he often wore a grogram coat, and the watered rum came to be called 'grog'. Often used (illegally) as currency in exchange for favours in quantities prescribed as 'sippers' and 'gulpers'. Additional issues of grog were made on the command 'splice the main brace' for celebrations or as a reward for performing especially onerous duties. The RN discontinued the practice of issuing rum in 1970. A sailor might repay a colleague for a favour by giving him part or all of his grog ration, ranging from 'sippers' (a small amount) via 'gulpers' (a larger quantity) to 'grounders' (the entire tot).

Groggy: Drunk from having consumed a lot of grog.

Ground: The bed of the sea.

Gunwale: The upper edge of the side of a boat or ship, where the deck meets the hull sides. Also spelled 'gunnel'.

Gybe: To change tack when running downwind by allowing the stern to pass through the wind, swinging the boom across to the opposite side. Can be violent and dangerous if uncontrolled. Also spelled 'jibe'.

H

Halyard or halliard: Originally, ropes used for hoisting a spar with a sail attached; today, a line used to raise the head of any sail.

Hammock: Canvas sheets, slung from the deckhead in mess decks, in which seamen slept. 'Lash up and stow' a piped command to tie up hammocks and stow them (typically) in racks inboard of the ship's side to protect crew from splinters from shot and provide a ready means of preventing flooding caused by damage.

Hank: A fastener attached to the luff of the headsail that attaches the headsail to the forestay. Typical designs include a bronze or plastic hook with a spring-operated gate, or a strip of cloth webbing with a snap fastener.

Harbour: A harbour or harbour, or haven, is a place where ships may shelter from the weather or are stored. Harbours can be man-made or natural.

Hardtack: A hard and long-lasting dry biscuit, used as food on long journeys. Also called ship's biscuit.

Hatchway, hatch: A covered opening in a ship's deck through which cargo can be loaded or access made to a lower deck; the cover to the opening is called a hatch.

Hawser: Large rope used for mooring or towing a vessel.

Head: 1. The toilet or latrine of a vessel, which in sailing ships projected from the bows. 2. The top edge of a sail.

Headsail: Any sail flown in front of the most forward mast.

Heave: A vessel's transient, vertical, up-and-down motion.

Heaving to: Stopping a sailing vessel by lashing the helm in opposition to the sails. The vessel will gradually drift to leeward, the speed of the drift depending on the vessel's design.

Heel: The lean or tilt of a sailing vessel to one side, caused by the force of the wind in the sails. Differs from 'list', which is caused by uneven weight distribution.

Helm: A ship's steering mechanism; see tiller and ship's wheel. The wheel and/or wheelhouse area. Also see wheelhouse.

Helmsman: A person who steers a ship.

Herring buss: A type of seagoing fishing vessel used by Dutch and Flemish herring fishermen from the 15th through the early 19th century.

Hitch: A type of knot used to attach a line to a spar, ring, post, or another line. Unlike a bend, a hitch secures to an object rather than joining two ropes.

Holiday: A gap in the coverage of newly applied paint, slush, tar or other preservative.

Hulk: 1. A ship, often an old ship or one that has become obsolete or uneconomical to operate, that has had its rigging or internal equipment removed and is incapable of going to sea, but that is afloat and continues to serve a useful function, such as providing living, office, training, storage, or prison space.

Hull: The shell and framework of the basic flotation-oriented part of a ship.

Hydrofoil: A boat with wing-like foils mounted on struts below the hull, lifting the hull entirely out of the water at speed and allowing water resistance to be greatly reduced.

I

Icing: A serious hazard where cold temperatures (below about -10°C) combined with high wind speed (typically force 8 or above on the Beaufort scale) result in spray blown off the sea freezing immediately on contact with the ship

Idlers: Members of a ship's company not required to serve watches. These were in general specialist tradesmen such as the carpenter and the sail maker.

In irons: When the bow of a sailboat is headed into the wind and the boat has stalled and is unable to manoeuvre.

Inboard motor: An engine mounted within the hull of a vessel, usually driving a fixed propeller by a shaft protruding through the stern. Generally used on larger vessels. Also see stern drive and outboard motor.

J

Jacob's ladder: A portable ladder of rope or chain, with wooden or metal rungs, lowered over the side of a vessel for boarding from the water or from a smaller craft.

Jetsam: Debris ejected from a ship that sinks or washes ashore. See also Flotsam.

Jetty: A man-made wall in open water rising several feet above high tide made of rubble and rocks used to create a breakwater, shelter, erosion control, a channel, or other such purpose.

Jib: A triangular staysail at the front of a ship.

Jibboom: A spar used to extend the bowsprit.

Jibe: See #Gybe.

Jury rig: Both the act of rigging a temporary mast and sails and the name of the resulting rig. A jury rig would be built at sea when the original rig was damaged, then it would be used to sail to a harbour or other safe place for permanent repairs.

K

Kedge: A technique for moving or turning a ship by using a relatively light anchor known as a kedge. The kedge anchor may be dropped while in motion to create a pivot and thus perform a sharp turn. The kedge anchor may also be carried away from the ship in a smaller boat, dropped, and then weighed, pulling the ship forward.

Kedge anchor: A secondary, lighter anchor used for manoeuvring, keeping a vessel from swinging, or warping the vessel to a new position.

Keel: The central structural basis of the hull

Keelhauling: Maritime punishment: to punish by dragging under the keel of a ship.

Killick: A small anchor. A fouled killick is the substantive badge of non-commissioned officers in the RN. Seamen promoted to the first step in the promotion ladder are called 'Killick'. The badge signifies that here is an Able Seaman skilled to cope with the awkward job of dealing with a fouled anchor.

Kissing the gunner's daughter: bend over the barrel of a gun for punitive beating with a cane or cat

Knockdown: The condition of a sailboat being pushed abruptly to horizontal, with the mast parallel to the water surface.

Knot: A unit of speed: 1 nautical mile (1.8520 km; 1.1508 mi) per hour. Originally speed was measured by paying out a line from the stern of a moving boat; the line had a knot every 47 feet 3 inches (14.40 m), and the number of knots passed out in 30 seconds gave the speed through the water in nautical miles per hour. Sometimes 'knots' is mistakenly stated as 'knots per hour,' but the latter is a measure of acceleration (i.e., 'nautical miles per hour per hour') rather than of speed.

Know the ropes: A sailor who 'knows the ropes' is familiar with the miles of cordage and ropes involved in running a ship.

L

Ladder: On board a ship, all 'stairs' are called ladders, except for literal staircases aboard passenger ships. Most 'stairs' on a ship are narrow and nearly vertical, hence the name. Believed to be from the Anglo-Saxon word hiaeder, meaning ladder.

Lagan: Debris that has sunk to the seabed.

Laid up: To be placed in reserve or mothballed. The latter usage is used in modern times and can refer to a specific set of procedures used by the US Navy to preserve ships in good condition.

Land lubber: A person unfamiliar with being on the sea.

Lanyard: A rope that ties something off.

Larboard: Obsolete term for the left side of a ship. Derived from 'lay-board' providing access between a ship and a quay, when ships normally docked with the left side to the wharf. Replaced by port side or port, to avoid confusion with starboard.

Lazarette: A storage compartment below deck, typically located in the stern of a yacht, used to stow gear such as fenders, mooring lines, and spare equipment.

Lead line: A weighted line marked at regular intervals, lowered to the seabed to measure water depth; the forerunner of the echo sounder. The lead was often greased to bring up a sample of the bottom.

League: A unit of length, normally equal to three nautical miles.

Lee: The side of the vessel or an object that is sheltered from the wind; the downwind side.

Lee shore: A shore downwind of a ship. A ship which cannot sail well to windward risks being blown onto a lee shore and grounded.

Lee side: The side of a ship sheltered from the wind (cf. weather side).

Leech: The aft or trailing edge of a fore-and-aft sail; the leeward edge of a spinnaker; a vertical edge of a square sail. The leech is susceptible to twist, which is controlled by the boom vang, mainsheet and, if rigged with one, the gaff vang.

Leeward: In the direction that the wind is blowing towards.

Leeway: The amount that a ship is blown leeward by the wind. See also weatherly.

Length overall, or LOA: The maximum length of a vessel's hull measured parallel to the waterline, usually measured on the hull alone, and including overhanging ends that extend beyond the main bow and main stern perpendicular members. For sailing vessels, this may exclude the bowsprit and other fittings added to the hull, but sometimes bowsprits are included.

Liberty: A relatively short period when a sailor is allowed ashore for recreation. See also shore leave.

Lifeline: A safety wire or rope rigged along the sides of a vessel's deck, supported by stanchions, to prevent crew from falling overboard.

List: A vessel's angle of lean or tilt to one side, in the direction called roll. Typically refers to a lean caused by flooding or improperly loaded or shifted cargo (as opposed to 'heeling', which see).

Loaded to the gunwales: Literally, having cargo loaded as high as the ship's rail; also means extremely drunk.

Log: 1. A device used to measure a vessel's speed through the water and the distance run. 2. The official daily record of a vessel's navigation, weather conditions, crew activities, and significant events.

Loggerhead: An iron ball attached to a long handle, used for driving caulking into seams and (occasionally) in a fight. Hence: 'at loggerheads'.

Loose cannon: An irresponsible and reckless individual whose behavior (either intended or unintended) endangers the group he or she belongs to. A loose cannon, weighing thousands of pounds, would crush anything and anyone in its path, and possibly even break a hole in the hull, thus endangering the seaworthiness of the whole ship.

Lubber's line: A mark on the inside of a compass bowl that indicates the fore-and-aft axis of the vessel, allowing the helmsman to read the course being steered.

Luffing: 1. When a sailing vessel is steered far enough to windward that the sail is no longer completely filled with wind (the luff of a fore-and-aft sail begins to flap first). 2.

Loosening a sheet so far past optimal trim that the sail is no longer completely filled with wind. 3. The flapping of the sail(s) which results from having no wind in the sail at all.

M

Main deck: The uppermost continuous deck extending from bow to stern.

Mainbrace: One of the braces attached to the mainmast.

Mainmast (or Main): The tallest mast on a ship.

Mainsheet: Sail control line that allows the most obvious effect on mainsail trim. Primarily used to control the angle of the boom, and thereby the mainsail, this control can also increase or decrease downward tension on the boom while sailing upwind, significantly affecting sail shape. For more control over downward tension on the boom, use a boom vang.

Making way: A vessel that is moving through the water under control — whether by sail, engine, or oars — as opposed to lying stopped or at anchor.

Man overboard!: A cry let out when a seaman has gone 'overboard' (fallen from the ship into the water).

Marines: Soldiers afloat. Royal Marines formed as the Duke of York and Albany's Maritime Regiment of Foot in 1664 with many and varied duties including providing guard to ship's officers should there be mutiny aboard. Sometimes thought by seamen to be rather gullible, hence the phrase 'tell it to the marines'.

Marlinspike: A tool used in rope work for tasks such as unlaying rope for splicing, untying knots, or forming a makeshift handle.

Mast: A vertical pole on a ship which supports sails or rigging. If a wooden, multi-part mast, this term applies specifically to the lowest portion.

Mast stepping: The process of raising the mast.

Masthead: The very top of a mast; the uppermost point. Instruments such as wind vanes, anemometers, and navigation lights are often fitted at the masthead.

Matelot: A traditional Royal Navy term for an ordinary sailor.

Mess: An eating place aboard ship. A group of crew who live and feed together,

Mizzenmast (or Mizzen): The third mast, or mast aft of the mainmast, on a ship.

Mole: A massive structure, usually of stone or concrete, used as a pier, a breakwater, or a causeway between places separated by water. May have a wooden structure built upon it and resemble a wooden pier or wharf, but a mole differs from a pier, quay, or wharf in that water cannot flow freely underneath it.

Moor: to attach a boat to a mooring buoy or post. Also, to dock a ship.

N

Nautical mile: a unit of length corresponding approximately to one minute of arc of latitude along any meridian arc. By international agreement it is exactly 1,852 metres (approximately 6,076 feet).

Neap tide: A tide occurring when the sun, Earth, and moon are at right angles, producing the smallest tidal range of the lunar cycle, with lower high tides and higher low tides than average.

No room to swing a cat: The entire ship's company was expected to witness floggings, assembled on deck. If it was very crowded, the bosun might not have room to swing the 'cat o' nine tails' (the whip).

O

Oakum: Material used for caulking hulls. Often hemp picked from old untwisted ropes.

Offing: the more distant part of the sea as seen from the shore and generally beyond anchoring ground.

Old man, (The): Crew's slang for the captain (master or commanding officer) of a vessel.

Old salt: Slang for an experienced mariner.

On the hard: A boat that has been hauled and is now sitting on dry land.

Ordinary: See in ordinary.

Outboard motor: A self-contained propulsion unit — engine, gearbox, and propeller — mounted on the outside of a vessel's transom and removable when not in use.

Outhaul: A line used to control the shape of a sail.

Outward bound: To leave the safety of port, heading for the open ocean.

Over the barrel: Adult sailors were flogged on the back or shoulders while tied to a grating, but boys were beaten instead on the posterior (often bared), with a cane or cat, while bending, often tied down, over the barrel of a gun, known as #Kissing the gunner's daughter.

Overbear: To sail downwind directly at another ship, stealing the wind from its sails.

Over-reaching: When tacking, holding a course too long.

Ox-eye: A cloud or other weather phenomenon that may be indicative of an upcoming storm.

P

Painter: A rope attached to the bow of a dinghy or small boat, used for towing, securing it alongside a larger vessel, or making fast at a dock.

Panting: The pulsation in and out of the bow and stern plating as the ship alternately rises and plunges deep into the water

Parley: a discussion or conference, especially between enemies, over terms of a truce or other matters.

Passageway: Hallway of a ship.

Pay off: To let a vessel's head fall off from the wind (to leeward.)

Pay out: To ease or let out a line or rope, increasing its length on the working side.

Paymaster: The officer responsible for all money matters in RN ships including the paying and provisioning of the crew, all stores, tools and spare parts. See also: purser.

Pendant: A length of wire or rope secured at one end to a mast or spar and having a block or other fitting at the lower end. Often used incorrectly when referring to a Pennant (flag).

Pennant: A long, thin triangular flag flown from the masthead of a military ship (as opposed to a burgee, the flags thus flown on yachts).

Pier: A raised structure, typically supported by widely spread piles or pillars, used industrially for loading and unloading commercial ships, recreationally for walking and housing attractions at a seaside resort, or as a structure for use by boatless fishermen. The lighter structure of a pier contrasts with the more solid foundations of a quay or the closely spaced piles of a wharf. In North America, the term 'pier' used alone connotes either a pier used (or formerly used) by commercial shipping or one used for fishing, while in Europe the term used alone connotes a recreational pier at a seaside resort.

Pilot: A person possessing detailed local knowledge of a particular stretch of coastline, harbour, or waterway who boards a vessel to guide it safely through those waters.

Pilotage: The practice of navigating coastal and harbour waters using visual landmarks, local charts, buoys, and depth soundings rather than celestial or open-ocean methods.

Pitch: The fore-and-aft rocking motion of a vessel, in which the bow rises and falls alternately; one of the three primary motions of a vessel at sea (the others being roll and yaw).

Planing: When a fast-moving vessel skims over the water instead of pushing through it.

Planing hull: A hull form designed to rise up and skim over the surface of the water at speed, rather than pushing through it; requires significant power to achieve planing speed.

Plimsoll line (also national Load Line): A special marking, positioned amidships, that indicates the draft of the vessel and the legal limit to which the vessel may be loaded for specific water types and temperatures.

Pontoon: A flat-bottomed vessel used as a ferry, barge, car float or a float moored alongside a jetty or a ship to facilitate boarding.

Poop deck: A high deck on the aft superstructure of a ship.

Port: The left side of the boat. Towards the left-hand side of the ship facing forward (formerly Larboard). Denoted with a red light at night.

Port side: The left side of a vessel when facing forward (toward the bow). Denoted by a red light at night.

Porthole or port: an opening in a ship's side, esp. a round one for admitting light and air, fitted with thick glass and, often, a hinged metal cover, a window

Press gang: Formed body of personnel from a ship of the Royal Navy (either a ship seeking personnel for its own crew or from a 'press tender' seeking men for a number of ships) that would identify and force (press) men, usually merchant sailors into service on naval ships usually against their will.

Prow: a poetical alternative term for bows.

Q

Quarterdeck: The aftermost deck of a warship. In the age of sail, the quarterdeck was the preserve of the ship's officers.

Quayside: Refers to the dock or platform used to fasten a vessel to

Queen's (King's) Regulations: The standing orders governing the British Royal Navy issued in the name of the current Monarch.

R

Radar: Acronym for RAdio Detection And Ranging. An electronic system designed to transmit radio signals and receive reflected images of those signals from a 'target' in order to determine the bearing and distance to the 'target'.

Ratlines: Rope ladders permanently rigged from bulwarks and tops to the mast to enable access to topmasts and yards.

Reaching: Sailing across the wind: from about 60° to about 160° off the wind. Reaching consists of 'close reaching' (about 60° to 80°), 'beam reaching' (about 90°) and 'broad reaching' (about 120° to 160°). See also beating and running.

Ready about: A call to indicate imminent tacking (see going about).

Reefer: 1. A shipboard refrigerator. 2. A refrigerated cargo ship, used to carry perishable goods that require refrigeration (also reefer ship)

Reeve: (Past tense rove) To thread a line through blocks in order to gain a mechanical advantage, such as in a block and tackle.

Regatta: A series of boat races, usually of sailboats or rowboats, but occasionally of powered boats.

Rhumb line: A course of constant compass bearing that, when plotted on a Mercator chart, appears as a straight line; used for practical navigation over moderate distances.

Roach: The convex curvature of the leech of a sail that extends beyond a straight line drawn from head to clew, increasing the sail area; often supported by battens.

Rode: The complete anchor assembly of line, chain, or combination thereof, connecting the anchor to the vessel.

Roll: The side-to-side rocking motion of a vessel about its fore-and-aft axis, caused by wave action or wind.

Rudder: A flat, hinged or pivoting blade mounted vertically at the stern below the waterline, which deflects water flow to steer the vessel.

Rummage sale: A sale of damaged cargo (from French arrimage).

Running rigging: The movable lines, ropes, and cables used to hoist, lower, and control the shape and angle of sails; contrasted with standing rigging, which is fixed.

S

Safe Harbour: A harbour which provides safety from bad weather

Safe Haven: A safe harbour, including natural harbours, which provide safety from bad weather or attack.

Safety harness: A harness worn by crew members that attaches via a tether to jacklines or fixed points on the vessel, preventing loss overboard in rough conditions.

Scantlings: Dimensions of ships structural members, e.g., frame, beam, girder, etc.

Scudding: A term applied to a vessel when carried furiously along by a tempest.

Sculling: A method of using oars to propel watercraft in which the oar or oars touch the water on both the port and starboard sides of the craft, or over the stern. On sailboats with transom-mounted rudders, forward propulsion can be made by a balanced side to side movement of the tiller, a form of sculling.

Scuppers: Originally a series of pipes fitted through the ships side from inside the thicker deck waterway to the topside planking to drain water overboard, larger quantities drained through freeing ports, which were openings in the bulwarks.

Scuttle: A small opening, or lid thereof, in a ship's deck or hull.

Scuttlebutt: 1. A barrel with a hole in used to hold water that sailors would drink from. By extension (in modern naval usage), a shipboard drinking fountain or water cooler. 2. Slang for gossip.

Sea chest: A watertight box built against the hull of the ship communicating with the sea through a grillage, to which valves and piping are attached to allow water in for ballast, engine cooling, and firefighting purposes. Also a wooden box used to store a sailor's effects.

Sea trial: The testing phase of a boat, ship, or submarine, usually the final step in her construction, conducted to measure a vessel's performance and general seaworthiness before her owners take delivery of her.

Seaboots: High waterproof boots for use at sea. In leisure sailing, known as sailing wellies.

Seacock: a valve in the hull of a boat.

Seaworthy: Certified for, and capable of, safely sailing at sea.

Sextant: Navigational instrument used to measure a ship's latitude.

Shackle: A U-shaped metal fitting, closed by a threaded pin or snap mechanism, used to connect ropes, chains, blocks, and other hardware.

Shakedown cruise: A cruise performed before a ship enters service or after major changes such as a crew change, repair, or overhaul during which the performance of the ship and her crew are tested under working conditions.

Shanghaied: Condition of a crewman involuntarily impressed into service on a ship.

Sheet: A rope used to control the setting of a sail in relation to the direction of the wind.

Shoal: Shallow water that is a hazard to navigation.

Shoal draught: Shallow draught, making the vessel capable of sailing in unusually shallow water.

Shroud: A rope or cable serving to hold a mast up from side to side.

Skeg: A downward or sternward projection from the keel in front of the rudder. Protects the rudder from damage, and in bilge keelers may provide one 'leg' of a tripod on which the boat stands when the tide is out.

Skiff: A small boat, traditionally a coastal or river craft, for leisure or fishing, with a single person or small crew. Sailing skiffs have developed into high performance competitive classes.

Skipper: The captain of a ship.

Skysail: A sail set very high, above the royals. Only carried by a few ships.

Skyscraper: A small, triangular sail, above the skysail. Used in light winds on a few ships.

Slack water: The brief period of minimal tidal current occurring at the turn of the tide, between ebb and flood; a favourable time to navigate tidal passages.

Slush: Greasy substance obtained by boiling or scraping the fat from empty salted meat storage barrels, or the floating fat residue after boiling the crew's meal. In the Royal Navy the perquisite of the cook who could sell it or exchange it (usually for alcohol) with other members of the crew. Used for greasing parts of the running rigging of the ship and therefore valuable to the master and bosun.

Slush fund: The money obtained by the cook selling slush ashore. Used for the benefit of the crew (or the cook).

Son of a gun: The Royal Navy sometimes had illegitimate children on board their ships. These children lived on the gun-deck and earned their keep by performing various useful duties.

Sound: 1. To measure the depth of water with a lead line or echo sounder. 2. A relatively narrow body of water between an island and the mainland, or between two bodies of water.

Spanker: A fore-and-aft or gaff-rigged sail on the aft-most mast of a square-rigged vessel and the main fore-and-aft sail (spanker sail) on the aft-most mast of a (partially) fore-and-aft rigged vessel such as a schooner, a barquentine, and a barque.

Spar: A wooden, in later years also iron or steel pole used to support various pieces of rigging and sails. The big five-masted full-rigged tall ship Preussen (German spelling: Preußen) had crossed 30 steel yards, but only one wooden spar — the little gaff of its spanker sail.

Spindrift: Finely divided water swept from crest of waves by strong winds.

Splice the mainbrace: A euphemism, it is an order given aboard naval vessels to issue the crew with a drink, traditionally grog. The phrase splice the mainbrace is used idiomatically meaning to go ashore on liberty, intending to go out for an evening of drinking.

Spring line: A mooring line led diagonally fore or aft from the vessel to a cleat on the dock, preventing the vessel from moving ahead or astern while alongside.

Spring tide: A tide occurring at or near new moon and full moon, when the gravitational forces of the sun and moon are aligned, producing a greater-than-average tidal range.

Square meal: A sufficient quantity of food. Meals on board ship were served to the crew on a square wooden plate in harbor or at sea in good weather. Food in the Royal Navy was invariably better or at least in greater quantity than that available to the average landsman. However, while square wooden plates were indeed used on board ship, there is no established link between them and this particular term. The OED gives the earliest reference from the U.S. in the mid 19th century.

Squared away: Yards held rigidly perpendicular to their masts and parallel to the deck. This was rarely the best trim of the yards for efficiency but made a pretty sight for inspections and in harbor. The term is applied to situations and to people figuratively to mean that all difficulties have been resolved or that the person is performing well and is mentally and physically prepared.

Standing rigging: The fixed wires, rods, or cables that support the mast and do not normally move during sailing; includes stays and shrouds.

Starboard: The right side of a vessel when facing forward (toward the bow). Denoted by a green light at night.

Stern: The aft-most section of a vessel's hull.

Swinging the lead: 1. Measuring the depth of water beneath a ship using a lead-weighted sounding line. Regarded as a relatively easy job, thus: 2. Feigning illness etc to avoid a hard job.

T

Tabernacle: A large bracket attached firmly to the deck, to which the foot of the mast is fixed. It has two sides or cheeks and a bolt forming the pivot around which the mast is raised and lowered.

Tack: 1. The lower forward corner of a fore-and-aft sail, attached to the mast or boom. 2. The course a sailing vessel is on relative to the wind; a vessel on starboard tack has the wind coming from its right side. 3. The manoeuvre of turning the bow of a vessel through the wind to change course.

Taffrail: A rail at the stern of the boat that covers the head of the counter timbers.

Tailshaft: A kind of metallic shafting (a rod of metal) to hold the propeller and connected to the power engine. When the tailshaft is moved, the propeller may also be moved for propulsion.

Taken aback: An inattentive helmsmen might allow the dangerous situation to arise where the wind is blowing into the sails 'backwards', causing a sudden (and possibly dangerous) shift in the position of the sails.

Taking the wind out of his sails: To sail in a way that steals the wind from another ship. cf. overbear.

Tattle Tale: Light cord attached to a mooring line at two points a few inches apart with a slack section in between (resembling an inch-worm) to indicate when the line is stretching from the ship's rising with the tide. Obviously only used when moored to a fixed dock or pier and only on watches with a flood tide.

Tell-tale (sometimes tell-tail): A light piece of string, yarn, rope or plastic (often magnetic audio tape) attached to a stay or a shroud to indicate the local wind direction. They may also be attached to the surface and/or the leech of a sail to indicate the state of the air flow over the surface of the sail. They are referenced when optimizing the trim of the sails to achieve the best boat speed in the prevailing wind conditions. (See Dogvane)

Three sheets to the wind: On a three-masted ship, having the sheets of the three lower courses loose will result in the ship meandering aimlessly downwind. Also, a sailor who has drunk strong spirits beyond his capacity.

Tide: The periodic rise and fall of sea levels caused primarily by the gravitational attraction of the moon, and to a lesser extent the sun, on the Earth's oceans.

Tiller: A horizontal lever attached directly to the top of the rudder post, used to steer smaller vessels by hand.

Toe the line or Toe the mark: At parade, sailors and soldiers were required to stand in line, their toes in line with a seam of the deck.

Topgallant: The mast or sails above the tops.

Topman: A crewmember stationed in a top.

Touch and go: 1. The bottom of the ship touching the bottom, but not grounding. 2. Stopping at a dock or pier for a very short time without tying up, to let off or take on crew or goods.

Transom: The aft 'wall' of the stern; often the part to which an outboard unit or the drive portion of a sterndrive is attached. A more or less flat surface across the stern of a vessel. Dinghies tend to have almost vertical transoms, whereas yachts' transoms may be raked forward or aft.

Trimaran: A vessel with three hulls.

Trimmer, sometimes Coal trimmer: person responsible for ensuring that a vessel remains in 'trim' (that the cargo and fuel are evenly balanced). An important task on a coal-fired vessel, as it could get 'out-of-trim' coal is consumed.

Turtleback deck: A deck that has slight positive curvature when viewed in cross-section. The purpose of this curvature is usually to shed water, but in warships it also functions to make the deck more resistant to shells.

Turtling: The condition of a sailboat's (in particular a dinghy's) capsizing to a point where the mast is pointed straight down and the hull is on the surface resembling a turtle shell.

U

Unassisted sailing: A voyage, usually single-handed, with no intermediate port stops or physical assistance from external sources.

Under the weather: Serving a watch on the weather side of the ship, exposed to wind and spray.

V

Vang: 1. A rope (line) leading from gaff to either side of the deck, used to prevent the gaff from sagging. 2. See #Boom vang.

Vanishing angle: The maximum degree of heel after which a vessel becomes unable to return to an upright position.

VHF radio: Very High Frequency marine radio, the primary means of short-range communication between vessels and shore stations; Channel 16 is the international distress, urgency, and safety calling channel.

W

Waft: A signal flag on a vessel.

Waist: the central deck of a ship between the forecastle and the quarterdeck.

THE END